Emotional Intelligence for Parents and Kids

Table of Contents

Chapter 1. Introduction

Welcome to a vibrant journey that aims to light the path towards emotional wellness for you and your children alike! Our Special Report on Emotional Intelligence for Parents and Kids is designed to serve as your jolly companion, unraveling the wonders of emotional intelligence and its vital role in parenting and nurturing resilient kids. Get ready to dive into a sea of knowledge, stirring narratives, practical strategies, and heartwarming anecdotes that are bound to inspire. Captivating from the first line and insightful until the last; it's more than a report, it's a transformative experience for your family unit. Intrigued? Prepare to embark on an enlightening adventure, because this Special Report is the ticket to an emotionally awakened and harmonious home. You won't just want to buy it, you'll want to cherish it!

Chapter 2. Understanding Emotional Intelligence

Ever wondered about the intangible forces that drive our understanding towards ourselves and others? Emotional intelligence defines those forces, depicted not so much in our IQ but manifested through our feelings, relationships, responses, and adaptability. Harnessing the power of emotional intelligence signifies unlocking the path to well-being, resilience, and overall balanced life not just for us but for our children too.

2.1. What is Emotional Intelligence?

Emotional Intelligence, or EI, refers to an individual's ability to discern, utilize, comprehend, and manage their own emotions in positive ways to relieve stress, communicate effectively, empathize with others, overcome challenges, and defuse conflict. It spans a broad set of skills which, when comprehended and applied, can aid in navigating efficiently through life's ups and downs.

The concept was popularized in 1995 by psychologist and author Daniel Goleman, but the groundwork for EI as it's understood today was laid by Peter Salovey and John Mayer's earlier work. They defined emotional intelligence as "the subset of social intelligence that involves the ability to monitor one's own and others' feelings and emotions, to discriminate among them and to use this information to guide one's thinking and actions."

2.2. Components of Emotional Intelligence

Goleman's model of EI identifies five key elements of emotional intelligence:

1. Self-awareness - Recognizing one's emotions and their impact. People high in emotional self-awareness know what they're feeling and why.

2. Self-regulation - Controlling one's emotions and impulses, those possessing this skill don't allow emotions to wreak havoc, they manage them astutely.

3. Motivation - Being driven to achieve for the sake of achievement, it's being passionate about one's goals irrespective of external rewards.

4. Empathy - Understanding the emotions of others, this quality helps in forming connections and understanding other's perspectives.

5. Social skills - Building good interpersonal relationships, it's about the art of navigating social complexities and building strong bonds.

2.3. The Importance of Emotional Intelligence

Why should we care about emotional intelligence? Crucially, research has found that EI plays an influential role in personal, academic and professional success. It impacts everything from our mental health to work performance, from how we view ourselves to how we interact with others.

The efficacy of EI is such that people with high emotional intelligence are more likely to be effective in their roles, exhibit leadership capabilities, demonstrate strong mental health, and possess a positive attitude. They are also adept at understanding and regulating their emotions, which in turn fosters resilience and decreases the probability of succumbing to stress-induced ailments.

In the context of children, nurturing emotional intelligence can set the foundation for success in every facet of their lives. Research indicates that children with high EI often perform better acadically, have better relationships, demonstrate better social skills, exhibit fewer behavioural issues, and have an improved sense of self-worth.

2.4. Emotional Intelligence in Parenting

The role of emotional intelligence in parenting can hardly be overstated. It lies at the heart of forming deep, loving relationships with our children, guiding them towards meaningful paths, and becoming a role model for them. By mastering emotional intelligence, parents can elevate their parenting practices, promoting empathy, love, understanding, and mutual respect, in turn boosting their child's emotional development.

When parents are aware of their emotional states and can manage them effectively, they can significantly impact their child's ability to develop their own emotional intelligence. Parents who exhibit warmth, sensitivity, and awareness of their own emotions are more likely to have kids who exhibit these facets too.

Moreover, understanding emotional intelligence in the context of parenting can have far-reaching effects including improved parent-child communication, effective conflict resolution, and healthy emotional expression. It can also aid parents in equipping children with the tools needed for emotional resilience, empathy, positivity, social skills, and stress management - critical elements of their emotional and social development.

2.5. Cultivating Emotional Intelligence

Given its importance, one might wonder: Is emotional intelligence innate, or can it be developed? The consensus affirms that while some individuals might naturally possess higher EI, these skills can be learned and cultivated.

Here are a few strategies:

1. Practice mindfulness: Mindfulness involves staying in the present moment, non-judgmentally. It aids in recognizing our feelings without being overpowered by them.

2. Open communication: Encourage open dialogue about emotions in the household. Make it normal to discuss feelings.

3. Empathy first: Practice empathetic responses. This not only aids in understanding others' emotions but models emotional regulation for children.

4. Encourage expression: Give children the space to express their emotions and validate their feelings. It's OK to feel.

5. Model emotional intelligence: Remember, children learn the most from observing their parents. Practice the EI skills you'd like them to adopt.

In closing, understanding emotional intelligence orients us towards a deeper knowledge of our intrinsic selves and the world around us. Whether employed in self-reflection, in forge deeper connections with others, or for nurturing emotionally literate children, EI is a vital life tool, embedded in our everyday experiences. Its potential to enhance life in a profoundly meaningful way makes its understanding and application utterly transformative.

Chapter 3. The Role of Parents in Emotional Learning

Parenting is no simple task. It encompasses the responsibility of fostering a nurturing environment that not only supports a child's physical growth but also paves the way for their emotional development. Emotional learning is a significant aspect of a child's developmental process, and parents play an undeniable role in shaping these foundational years.

3.1. Initial Exposure to Emotions

The home serves as a child's first playground for emotional exploration. Parents, therefore, become the 'ambassadors of emotions,' introducing their children to a range of feelings. Children learn to process emotions like joy, sorrow, anger, excitement, anxiety, and others through their observation of parents' emotions and reactions. They pick up subtle cues and implicitly internalize ways of emotional expression. Hence, it becomes essential for parents to exhibit emotional literacy - to identify, understand, and express their emotions in a balanced and adaptive fashion - that will become the blueprint for a child's emotional landscape.

3.2. Emotional Modeling

Through the principle of 'emotional modelling,' children often emulate their parents in their emotional responses. They instinctively mirror their parents' emotional reactions, learning ways to respond to different situations. If a parent reacts to a stressful situation with panic or aggression, the child is likely to perceive the situation as threatening and react similarly. On the contrary, if parents display calmness and resolution in face of adversity, they teach their children resilience and emotional regulation. This underpins the importance of parents regulating their emotions, as it sets a constructive model for the child to learn and follow.

3.3. The Power of Validation

Active listening and emotional validation form the building blocks of a child's emotional security. Parents are key in teaching their children to understand and articulate their feelings. By acknowledging and validating their children's feelings - even those perceived as negative - parents impart a sense of self-worth, validating their emotions rather than dismissing or ignoring them. This nurtures an emotionally supportive environment, fostering self-esteem and strength in the child, enabling them to confidently navigate their emotional lives.

3.4. Teaching Emotional Intelligence

Emotional Intelligence, coined by psychologists Peter Salovey and John Mayer, and popularized by Daniel Goleman, refers to one's ability to perceive, integrate, understand, and manage emotions. In the context of parenting, training children in Emotional Intelligence entails teaching them strategies to understand emotions, techniques of self-control, and skills to manage emotional interactions effectively. It's about cultivating empathy, nurturing the ability to name their feelings, and teaching the techniques of problem-solving during emotional crises.

3.5. Instilling Empathy

One of the crucial elements of Emotional Intelligence is empathy, the ability to understand and share the feelings of others. Parental actions and behaviors play a pivotal role in cultivating empathy in children. By modelling empathetic behavior and nurturing compassionate interactions, parents can instill in their children the values of understanding, kindness, and respect for others' feelings.

It is, without doubt, a colossal responsibility that parents shoulder. But in this challenge lies a beautiful opportunity - to nurture emotionally intelligent children who grow up to be understanding, resilient, and compassionate individuals. It is this journey that stands as a testament to the transcendent power of emotionally intelligent parenting, turning homes into cradles of emotional learning and growth.

In conclusion, parents play an indispensable role in their children's emotional learning. Shaping the emotional landscape of children requires patience, validation, emotional literacy, and empathy. By consciously embarking on this journey, parents can transform their homes into vibrant arenas of emotional understanding and growth, fostering resilient children, and building emotionally harmonious families.

Chapter 4. Building an Emotionally Intelligent Home

Our journey begins with acknowledging that our home environments are the initial school of life for our children. In these spaces, they learn about love, communication, conflict, forgiveness, resilience, and even about failure. It is crucial to create an environment where your child's emotional intelligence can blossom. Hence, this chapter will present a roadmap for building an emotionally intelligent home, providing practical insights from neuroscientists, psychologists and education experts, peppered with anecdotes from real-life experiences.

4.1. Understanding Emotional Intelligence

Emotional intelligence, as defined by psychologists Peter Salovey and John D. Mayer, is the ability to perceive, understand, manage, and use emotions in both ourselves and others constructively. It refers to not just understanding your own emotions, but also empathizing with the emotions of others, nurturing relationships, and making decisions based on this understanding and empathy.

Emotional intelligence is divided into four domains, as shown below:

- Self-awareness

- Self-management

- Social-awareness

- Relationship management

Understanding these domains forms the initial steps of nurturing an emotionally intelligent home.

4.2. Nurturing Self-awareness

Self-awareness is the bedrock of emotional intelligence. It is the ability to recognize and understand your moods, emotions, and drives, as well as their impact on others. It begins with creating a non-judgmental and safe space at home where one can express their feelings openly. Below are some strategies to enhance self-awareness:

- Encourage children and adults in your home to articulate their feelings regularly. Use emotion flashcards or emotion wheels to aid younger kids.

- Hosting regular check-ins to gauge the emotional temperature of the family can be beneficial.

- Cultivate journaling habits. It can help in understanding personal feelings and patterns.

4.3. Building Self-management

Self-management revolves around handling feelings so they are appropriate to the situation. It includes self-control, adaptability, initiative, and optimism. Here are some effective ways to promote self-management:

- Encourage your children to practice deep breathing, mindfulness, and relaxation techniques when they are feeling overwhelmed.

- Role-modeling calm behavior during stressful instances can serve as a powerful example.

- Provide opportunities for them to take personal responsibility for chores or tasks, teaching them important lessons about self-regulation and adaptability.

4.4. Cultivating Social-awareness

Social awareness is the ability to understand the emotional makeup of other people. It's about empathy – being aware of another person's feelings, needs, and concerns. Enhancing this facet of emotional intelligence involves:

- Encouraging children to role-play different social scenarios.

- Reading books that depict various emotional circumstances, and discuss them afterwards.

- Reinforcing the value of service and kindness to others. Participate in community service activities as a family to develop empathy.

4.5. Fostering Relationship Management

This is the last domain of emotional intelligence. It involves managing emotions in others, inspiring others, influencing others, developing others, initiating or managing change, conflict management, building bonds, teamwork and collaboration.

- Engage in cooperative games that encourage teamwork and understanding.

- Establish clear family rules and consequences for unacceptable behaviors, ensuring that everybody respects them.

- Teach problem-solving skills and encourage your children to resolve their conflicts peacefully.

4.6. Developing an Emotionally Intelligent Environment

Creating a safe, accepting, and understanding emotional climate at home is key to fostering emotional intelligence. This involves parents modeling emotional intelligence themselves. Show empathy towards your child as well as the others around you, manage your own emotions in a healthy and adaptive manner, use emotional moments as opportunities for connection and teaching, and openly discuss feelings and emotional experiences.

Building an emotionally intelligent home can't happen overnight. It requires patience, continuous effort, love, and consistency. Remember that the goal is to raise children who can navigate the often-rough waters of emotions and emerge stronger, a tad wiser, and deeply compassionate. With effort and commitment, you can see this vision become a reality, contributing to a more empathetic world.

In the next chapter, we will give you practical tools and tips that can make this journey easier and enjoyable for you and your kids. So stay tuned!

Chapter 5. Nurturing Kids' Emotional Resilience

Just as we strive to adopt a balanced diet and regular exercise for physical wellbeing, developing emotional resilience is crucial in safeguarding our mental health. Given our fast-paced lives and the constant evolution of modern society, it's crucial to nurture this resilience in our kids from an early age, as it builds their capacity to adapt and thrive under any circumstances.

5.1. Understanding Emotional Resilience

Emotional resilience denotes the capability to heal, persevere, and recover from adversities. It is not about preventing stress or hardships but fostering a mindset and skills set to cope with, and rise above, challenges. For children, emotional resilience is an essential ingredient in being able to navigate the complex world they live in.

For parents, instilling emotional resilience in their children isn't about shielding them from life's difficulties. On the contrary, it involves helping them face these challenges head-on, encouraging them to see them as opportunities to learn, grow, and strengthen their emotional core.

Indeed, resilience is much more than just bouncing back. It's about building upon the experience and coming out stronger on the other side - the proverbial silver lining behind every cloud.

5.2. The Importance of Emotional Resilience

Emotional resilience helps children manage their feelings effectively, culminating in a better understanding of themselves and those around them. It supports children in maintaining control and balance in their lives, which is particularly vital in times of rapid change and uncertainty.

Resilient children are better equipped to handle tough situations — they are able to operate under stress, face setbacks head-on, and interpret adverse circumstances as manageable, rather than threatening.

Moreover, building resilience in children can lead to a number of positive outcomes, including greater confidence, improved problem-solving skills, better interpersonal relationships, enhanced academic performance, and overall sound physical and mental health.

5.3. Prerequisites to Building Emotional Resilience

Understanding emotions lies at the heart of nurturing emotional resilience. Parents should start by creating an environment where children can freely express their feelings without reprisal. Actively listening to your children's problems and acknowledging their emotions give them the much-needed assurance that their feelings matter.

Helping children understand their emotions involves assisting them in identifying what emotions they are feeling, why they are feeling them, and how they can respond appropriately. This may require active coaching on the parents' part.

Encourage them to articulate their emotional states and offer interpretations if they struggle. It's also crucial to focus on the emotional tone in your response, as it provides a model for your child on how to manage emotions and stay calm. It's okay if you don't have all the answers. The key is to empathize, reassure them and establish that it's natural to feel a certain way.

5.4. Strategies to Foster Emotional Resilience

Building resilience is an ongoing process that requires a multifaceted, consistent approach. Here are some strategies parents could consider.

5.4.1. Emotion Coaching

Emotion coaching is a five-step method for dealing with children's emotions. The steps include tuning in to your child's emotions, connecting with them, listening to them, naming the emotion, and finding good solutions. This method helps children learn about their emotions and how to manage them effectively.

5.4.2. Encouraging Problem-Solving

Teach your children to identify problems clearly, brainstorm potential solutions, weigh pros and cons, choose a solution, and evaluate the outcome. This process will not only help children to handle their current issues but will also equip them better for future challenges.

5.4.3. Being a Good Role Model

Children tend to mirror their parents' behavior and actions. Thus, demonstrating resilience in your own life will significantly affect your children's approach towards managing their emotions and dealing with adversities.

5.4.4. Fostering Optimism

Instill a positive mindset within your kids by praising their efforts, not just achievements. Promote positive thinking, problem-solving mentality, and appreciation for their accomplishments. This will encourage them to consider setbacks as temporary hurdles and not dead-ends.

5.4.5. Cultivating Strong Relationships

Having strong, supportive relationships helps children navigate the difficult periods in their lives. Encourage your children to build robust social networks and engage regularly in collaborative activities.

Chapter 6. Conclusion

Nurturing emotional resilience in children is not a one-off task. It's an ongoing process that develops as the child grows. As a parent, your nurturing, guidance, and patience are crucial in instilling and fostering resilience in your children. Remember, the goal isn't to create an unshakable, emotion-free child, but a child who can understand, articulate, manage, and learn from their emotions, transforming them into strengths to build upon. Be the supportive pillar they lean on, the coach they trust, and walk with them on the path leading towards emotional resilience. The journey may be long, but the destination—a resilient, emotionally intelligent, and mentally strong child— certainly makes it worthwhile.

Chapter 7. Emotion Coaching: A Step-by-Step Guide

Emotion coaching is an essential tool for parents to handle their children's emotional episodes, not as problems, but as opportunities for teaching. It involves understanding emotions, communicating about them effectively, and having the ability to handle them appropriately. This guide provides a step-by-step approach to becoming an emotion coaching parent.

7.1. Understanding Emotion Coaching

Emotion coaching begins with an understanding of why it's necessary. At the heart of this parenting style lies the belief that every emotion is valid. Emotions are direct responses to our experiences, and as such, they provide us with valuable information about ourselves and the world around us.

As humans, we're capable of experiencing a wide range of emotions–happiness, sadness, anger, excitement, and many more. Children, like adults, face an array of emotions, but unlike adults, they don't have the skills or understanding to manage these emotions effectively. This is where emotion coaching comes into play.

As an emotion coaching parent, one can guide their children through upsetting situations, teaching them how to understand and cope with their feelings. The long-run outcome of such potent exercises is raising emotionally intelligent kids who can navigate through life's ups and downs with confidence and resilience.

7.2. Why Emotion Coaching Matters

While it might seem easier as parents to brush aside children's emotional outbursts, doing so can stunt their emotional growth. Emotional intelligence – the ability to understand, use, and manage our emotions – impacts many areas of life, including relationships, academics, and mental health. Children who are not coached about their feelings struggle to identify and manage their emotions, leading to emotional outbursts, social problems, and even affecting their academic performance.

On the other hand, children who have had their emotions validated and guided are more likely to develop emotional intelligence. They become competent at understanding their own feelings, empathizing with others, and handling emotional situations, making them more resilient.

7.3. The Five Steps of Emotion Coaching

Emotion coaching can be distilled into five key steps. Each step offers a different insight that helps your child handle their emotional world.

7.3.1. Step 1: Be Emotionally Aware

Awareness is a crucial first step. Parents must be aware of their own emotions and understand that their responses to certain situations shape their children's emotional perceptions. Additionally, recognizing your child's emotions, both verbal and non-verbal, will help in responding appropriately.

7.3.2. Step 2: Recognize Emotion as an Opportunity for Connection or Teaching

Every emotional response presents a teaching or connection opportunity. Responding to your child's distress with empathy creates a sense of understanding and provides a chance to explore and discuss these feelings.

7.3.3. Step 3: Listen Empathetically and Validate Your Child's Feelings

Once you understand your child's emotion, show them empathy. Validate and respect their feelings irrespective of whether you agree or not. This validation makes them feel understood and acknowledged, creating a safe space for them to express themselves.

7.3.4. Step 4: Help Your Child Label Their Emotions

While children might experience a wide range of emotions, they might not have the vocabulary to identify them correctly. Help your children by giving a name to their feelings. This step will increase their emotional vocabulary and make it easier for them to express themselves in the future.

7.3.5. Step 5: Set Limits While Helping to Problem Solve

Emotion coaching does not mean permissive parenting. While validating and acknowledging your child's emotions, it's also essential to set limits and teach them appropriate ways to express these feelings. This means engaging with them in problem-solving to identify what they can do the next time they encounter such emotions.

7.4. Practical Strategies for Each Step

Emotion coaching is not an inborn skill, but it can certainly be learned and honed over time. A few practical strategies can assist parents in each step of this process:

7.4.1. Be Emotionally Aware

As a parent, note your emotional reactions to different situations. Reflect on them and understand what triggers certain emotions in you. Notice and interpret your child's verbal and non-verbal emotional cues correctly. These cues might include facial expressions, body language, or change in behavior.

7.4.2. Recognize Emotion as a Teaching Opportunity

See the emotional outburst not as a behavioral problem but as an opportunity to teach your child about emotions. Understand that when children express their feelings, they are reaching out for help or seeking comfort. Respond accordingly, and use these instances as teaching moments.

7.4.3. Listen Empathetically

Engage in active listening. Make eye contact, use comforting touches, and reassure your child that it's okay to have feelings. Use phrases like "I understand," "It sounds tough," etc., to convey your empathy.

7.4.4. Label Emotions

Help your child define what they're feeling. For example, if your child is upset because they can't play with a toy, you can say, "I see that you're upset because you can't play with the toy right now."

7.4.5. Set Limits and Problem Solve

Once you've validated your child's feelings and helped them label it, discuss what is acceptable behavior regardless of emotions. For example, "I understand you're angry, but it's not okay to hit." Then, brainstorm on how they can manage these feelings next time.

7.5. Incorporating Emotion Coaching Into Daily Activities

As much as it might seem like a rigorous task, emotion coaching can be incorporated into everyday activities, such as during playtime, meal times, bedtime, or while reading stories. Use these everyday situations as platforms to discuss emotions and make emotion coaching a natural part of your parenting.

Emotion coaching paves the way to a deeper understanding of ourselves and others. As parents, by exploring this path, you equip your children with a toolkit that not only benefits their childhood but impacts their adult life positively. Remember, it's never too late to become an emotion coaching parent. With patience and practice, you can foster an emotionally healthy environment at home.

Chapter 8. Empathy: The Heart of Emotional Intelligence

An inception of empathy, as a concept, binds us together – as parents, children, and humans. It's the fuel that powers our compassionate responses; it's the bridge that connects us to others, stitching individuals into communities, and communities into a cohesive societal fabric.

8.1. The Fabric of Empathy

Profoundly, empathy is the ability to understand and share the feelings of someone else, treading in their shoes and seeing the world through their lens. First and foremost, let's establish a clear distinction between sympathy and empathy — they are different. Sympathy is a feeling of pity or sadness for the suffering of others. Empathy, however, spans much deeper waters. It's not merely feeling 'for' others, but feeling 'with' them.

Children are not born with an in-built moral compass. Instead, they are taught and mentored to mold their emotional reactions, sympathetic responses, and empathetic understandings. As such, it's in your nurturing hands as a parent to help your child shape their empathy.

8.2. Empathy: A Multi-Faceted Gem

Empathy is an intricate concept that actually houses two distinct types: emotional empathy and cognitive empathy. Emotional empathy is quite instinctual, it's the ability to identify with someone's emotional state. For instance, a toddler may start crying upon seeing another child in distress, mirroring that child's emotion even though they do not fully comprehend the ordeal. This is emotional empathy at work.

Cognitive empathy, on the other hand, requires a greater degree of mental gymnastics. It involves understanding someone else's feelings and thoughts, even when they might differ from one's own. This type goes beyond feeling a person's plight to appreciating their perspective, even if it's contrary to your own understanding or belief.

8.3. Cultivating Empathy in Children

Empathy is cultivated through lived experiences and the conscious efforts of parents. Here are some practical strategies to nurture empathy in your little ones:

1. Role Modeling: Children learn by observing their parents. Display empathy in your interactions with others, and your child is likely to mirror this behavior. Show them that it's okay to discuss emotions and feelings and make empathetic responses a norm in your household.

2. Empathizing with Your Child: Show empathy towards your children's feelings. Validate their emotions by acknowledging them, and refrain from dismissing or minimizing their feelings.

3. Encourage Perspective-Taking: Engage your child in activities that promote perspective-taking. Reading books, watching movies, and discussing different characters' feelings can be effective ways to practice empathy.

4. Use Teachable Moments: Everyday situations offer a surplus of teachable moments. Point out instances of empathy in real life and explain the importance of showing compassion towards others.

8.4. The Mirror of Empathy: Emotional Intelligence

Integral to emotional intelligence, empathy plays multiple roles. It builds interpersonal relationships, fosters effective communication, enhances emotional awareness, and nurtures our innate altruism. Empathy is the platform on which emotional intelligence stands, the mirror that reflects the emotional realities of others.

When children are taught to be emotionally intelligent, they develop an emotional toolbox. This toolbox allows children to handle their emotions better, recognize others' feelings, and respond to these feelings appropriately.

8.5. A Case Study: Empathy in Play

Consider a typical school playground scene. A child trips, falls, and begins to cry. Another child, who is emotionally intelligent, notices these signs of distress. They empathetically offer comfort and help—even though they weren't involved in the incident. This intervention would likely calm the fallen child down, dissolve a potential conflict, and create a supportive environment. This is empathy in action, fuelled by emotional intelligence.

8.6. In Conclusion: Sowing the Seeds of Empathy

It's important to remember that fostering empathy is more of a journey than a destination. It isn't something that your child will master overnight, or even in a few weeks. But as a parent, you have the power to sow the seeds of empathy now. Your patience, understanding, and determination will eventually bear the fruit of an empathetic, emotionally intelligent child.

In the end, empathy brings us closer to the ideal of an emotionally harmonious home and community. It's the heart of emotional intelligence, the starting point of understanding, the underpinning of compassion, and the catalyst for social consciousness. By fostering empathy, we can hope to create a brighter, kinder, and more empathetic world for our children to flourish in. And isn't that the ultimate goal of parenting?

Chapter 9. Communication: The Bridge of Emotional Understanding

The intricacies of emotional intelligence cannot be discussed without encountering communication as the foundational stepping stone. A profound link exists between nurturing emotional intelligence and effective communication within households. The journey towards developing emotional understanding in our children starts by fostering a bridge of emotional communication, encouraging allowance for open dialogues, emotional teaching and learning opportunities, and strength-building interactions.

9.1. Navigating the Vast Ocean of Emotions

Before delving into strategies for effective emotional communication, let's first embark on a brief journey into the inner workings of emotions. Emotions are not just vague and abstract feelings; they are complex reactions to our perceptions and experiences, composed of physiological responses, subjective experiences, expressive behaviors, and goal-oriented actions. Understanding this robust architecture is crucial for parents aiming to enhance emotional intelligence in their children and themselves.

9.2. Discerning Emotions: The Basics

A critical part of communicating about emotions stems from understanding and identifying what we feel. Recognizing emotions within oneself and others and expressing them accurately is, in essence, the language of emotional intelligence. This language is how we give voice to our inner experiences, translating them into a tangible form that can be shared or even taught to our children. Encourage your kids to articulate their feelings from an early age and validate their emotions, helping to lay the foundations for a solid emotional understanding.

9.3. Deeper Connections through Active Listening

Active listening presents a transformative tool for enhancing emotional communication. As parents, when we listen–truly listen–to what our children say, we validate their feelings and experiences, which can foster deep emotional understanding. Actively ensure your children know that their emotions, thoughts, and ideas matter to you. Respond to their feeling vocalizations thoughtfully, provide comfort during distress, and celebrate during moments of joy.

9.4. Building an Emotional Vocabulary

Give a name to your child's emotions to assist their growth in emotional intelligence. Encourage them to expand upon these feelings and events that trigger them, fostering a rich emotional vocabulary. This practice not only helps children express their emotions better but also helps them understand and empathize with others' feelings.

```
[NOTE]
====
Dear Parents,
Remember that every small effort counts. It's okay if
the progress seems slow. Keep nurturing their emotional
lexicon, and over time, the expansion will surprise you.
```

9.5. Storytelling and Emotional Understanding

Storytelling serves as a powerful tool to promote emotional understanding. Reading stories about different characters, discussing their feelings, motivations, and actions, can prove beneficial in the development of a child's emotional intelligence. As we explore these narratives, we encourage our children to empathize and resonate with the characters.

9.6. Non-Verbal Communication: Untold Stories

While spoken language is a key part of emotional communication, non-verbal cues hold their own unique insights. Body language, facial expressions, gestures, tone of voice – all of these elements communicate volumes about what we feel. By educating children on these underlying messages, we not only enable them to understand non-verbal cues when they interact with others but also allow them to express themselves more fully.

9.7. Responding to Emotional Backlashes

Even the most emotionally adept individuals can experience intense or overwhelming emotions that may result in emotional backlashes. During such times, it is crucial to heighten our empathetic communication, help our children label their feelings, allow them to tell their story, and offer them comfort and reassurances.

9.8. Emotional Intelligence: Parents Set the Stage

Parents function as a child's primary emotional role model. Your approach to your own emotions provides a blueprint for your children to decipher their emotions. It's essential to exhibit emotional intelligence through your actions and express your feelings openly and appropriately. Practice the very lessons you aim to impart, for your actions bear more weight than mere words.

In conclusion, communication creates the bridge for understanding emotions in ourselves and others. Emotionally astute communication can ultimately foster an environment where everyone feels heard, understood, and loved. By prioritizing openness, empathy, and understanding in each interaction, we set our families on a course towards overall emotional health and resilience. It is a journey that has no quick fixes, and no destination - every day brings a promise of new emotional landscapes to navigate cleanly.

```
[IMPORTANT]
====
Conquering emotional communication strengthens the bonds
of our relationships, building resilience and capacity
to handle life□s trials more effectively. It's not just
about nurturing resilience in your children, but also
honing your emotional intelligence.
====
```

Remember, emotional intelligence breeds success not only acadically, but more importantly in life. Keep nurturing, keep expressing, and keep exploring this exciting domain of emotions. Let's build that bridge together. Let's foster a better future, hand-in-hand.

Chapter 10. Equipping Kids with Emotional Problem-Solving Skills

The foundation for equipping our children with emotional problem-solving skills comes from understanding that emotions aren't the opposition, but rather a normal and healthy part of being a human. Too often, we are told to suppress or hide our feelings, fostering an environment that creates emotional confusion. This understanding has never been more crucial, as today's kids navigate unknown waters. Now, let's journey through the various aspects of developing emotional problem-solving skills in kids.

10.1. Understanding Emotions

Understanding emotions is a fundamental first step. It involves recognizing and labeling emotions correctly, both in oneself and others. Even as we adults sometimes struggle to identify our feelings, it is equally challenging, if not more so, for children.

Breaking it down into relatable instances and stories aids in grasping the complexity. Narrate incidents where emotions come into play - the disappointment of a lost game, the exhilaration of an achieved goal, the fear of a nightmare, and the calmness of a quiet morning. Allow children to associate events with emotions, making it more recognizable.

10.2. Talking About Emotions

After recognizing emotions, the next stage involves discussing feelings openly. This step is crucial in educating children about the validity and normality of all emotions. Encourage regular conversations about feelings; you might ask, "How did that make you feel?" or propose, "I would have felt sad in that situation, would you?"

These discussions can also include fascinating insights on how different people may experience similar situations differently. Exploring such diversity of emotional responses can foster empathy and understanding.

10.3. Managing Emotions

Now that we have a grasp on identifying emotions, and we encourage open dialogues about them, managing emotions is the subsequent pillar to solidify. This part, often overlooked, is fundamental to emotional problem-solving skills.

Children must understand that emotions, though powerful, can be controlled. Methods may include calm breathing strategies, engaging in quiet activities such as reading or drawing, or physical tactics like running or yelling into a pillow.

It's important that children have a set of 'go-to' strategies tailored to them, allowing for autonomy and empowering them to control their emotional responses.

10.4. Emotional Problem-solving

Having laid foundations in identifying, discussing, and managing emotions, we're ready to delve into the core - Emotional Problem-Solving. The magnitude and gravity of this skill cannot be overemphasized – it's a life skill that proves essential across all ages and stages of life.

Encourage your children to approach their emotional problems as they would a math problem or a challenging puzzle. This approach allows children to step outside the whirlpool of emotions they're experiencing and consider them from a more detached, problem-solving perspective.

It starts with identifying the problem: what caused the onset of these emotions? Next, brainstorm possible solutions. Encourage your child to conjure as many solutions as they can, no matter how far-fetched they may seem.

Next comes evaluation. Discuss the potential consequences of each of the devised solutions. Finally, decide on a solution and enforce it. Encourage your child to monitor if the solution works or if there's a need for a new one.

10.5. Educating Through Role-Playing

Role-playing is one of the most effective strategies to teach emotional problem-solving skills. It's experiential learning in a controlled environment and presents an opportunity to rehearse emotional responses.

Set up simple scenarios that instigate certain emotional responses. Now switch roles, giving your child a chance to both experience and observe varied emotional responses. Discuss what could have been done differently and how different reactions could have affected the outcome.

10.6. Practice, Practice, and More Practice

Much like any other powerful skill, emotional problem-solving abilities come with practice. As your child comes across hurdles and obstacles, use them as teachable moments. Following the problem-solving approach every time imprints the pattern, making it a valuable habit.

Remember, the goal isn't to escape or avoid emotions, but to create a healthy emotional landscape where feelings can be freely and constructively expressed and discussed. This emotional embodiment equips children with mechanisms to cope with life's challenges.

To foster emotional intelligence and resilience into the core of our growing kids is no short-term task. But it is an enlightening and worthwhile journey. With love, patience, and a firm dedication to diving into this oceanic endeavor, your commitment will empower your children with a tool that leads to a deeper understanding of themselves and others, establishing an enduring sense of emotional balance. This is a ticket to a welcoming home - a home of empathy, resilience, and emotional wellness.

Remember! *Continuous consultation, effective communication, and honest reflection are your reliable companions on this journey.*

Chapter 11. Parents and Kids: Emotional Conflicts and Resolution

When we think about the parent-child bond, we might visualize a constant loop of love, affection, and mutual understanding. However, in the real world—despite the deep-rooted affection—this relationship often crosses paths with emotional conflicts. This chapter aims to guide parents through these challenging conflicts, providing them with practical strategies and tools to effectively manage and resolve them, fostering emotional intelligence in the process.

11.1. Understanding the Gap

Before we step into problem-solving, it's essential to comprehend the origin of these conflicts. A large part of parenting successes and stumbling blocks centers around the generational and emotional gap. Both parenting styles and children's emotional makeup are influenced by the times and circumstances in which they grow up. This generational gap can lead to misunderstanding or miscommunication, which may end up sparking emotional conflicts.

Understanding your child's emotions and coaching them to empathize with others form the basic framework needed to bridge this gap. By recognizing and managing their emotions, and by developing emotional intelligence, foundation can be developed for resolution of attentional conflicts.

11.2. Emotional Intelligence: The Core Tool

Emotional Intelligence (EI) is the ability to recognize, comprehend, and manage our emotions, and to do the same for others' emotions. Enhancing this ability plays a monumental role in resolving parent-child emotional conflicts and fostering healthier relationships. Emotional Intelligence can be compartmentalized into five core components—Self-awareness, Self-regulation, Motivation, Empathy, and Social Skills—all of which are vital threads in the fabric of effective conflict resolution.

11.3. The Five Components and Conflict Resolution

Let's delve into each component to see how they influence conflict resolution between parents and kids.

Self-Awareness: Being aware of one's emotions, their triggers, and how they influence behavior is the first step towards conflict resolution. By understanding their emotions, parents and children can communicate feelings more effectively, reducing misunderstandings that lead to conflicts.

Self-Regulation: This is the ability to manage and control emotionally charged reactions. A crucial skill for de-escalating tense situations and maintaining a calm environment, it prevents conflicts from spiralling out of control.

Motivation: An intrinsic drive to achieve, and a positive approach towards life, can help both parents and children navigate emotional conflicts constructively. A motivated individual is more likely to address conflicts optimistically, shaping a positive family environment.

Empathy: Perhaps the most vital tool, empathy encourages understanding and sharing of others' feelings. If parents can empathize with their children and vice versa, it fosters mutual respect and understanding, reducing the scope for emotional conflict significantly.

Social Skills: Successful conflict resolution often requires refined social skills, like effective communication, active listening, and problem-solving. Developing these skills can help families navigate through emotional conflicts healthily and constructively.

11.4. Practical Techniques for Resolving Emotional Conflicts

Applying the principles of emotional intelligence for conflict resolution may seem daunting initially. However, practical tactics can make the process less overwhelming.

Active Listening: Encourage your child to express themselves and listen without interruption or judgement. This conveys that you value their feelings, fostering open communication essential for resolving differences.

Understanding the Root Cause: If conflicts are recurring, there might be underlying issues at play. Dig deeper to understand the root cause, which allows you to address the problem directly.

Show Empathy: Show your child that you understand and share their feelings. Exhibiting empathy not only makes your child feel valued but also teaches them to empathize with others—an important tool in conflict resolution.

Negotiation and Compromise: Work collaboratively with your child to arrive at a solution that satisfies both parties. This approach reinforces the importance of fairness and compromise in conflict resolution.

Solution-focused Approach: Instead of focusing on the problem or who is to blame, center conversations around potential solutions. This approach ensures that conflicts are resolved constructively, emphasizing learning and growth.

Remember that helping your child develop emotional intelligence and effective conflict resolution skills is a long-term process. There will be successes and setbacks. But each experience is a stepping stone towards building a solid foundation of emotional competence and harmony in your child's life, cascading to an emotionally aware home environment.

Chapter 12. Sustaining Emotional Wellness: A Lifelong Endeavor

Emotional wellness is not an overnight victory, rather, it's a lifelong journey of self-discovery, personal development, and continuous learning. It's about understanding and managing not only your emotions but, in the context of parenthood, also those of your children. Embracing this journey paves the way for mature emotional intelligence, trust-building, and lays a sturdy foundation for a harmonious and understanding family environment.

12.1. Understanding Emotional Wellness

Emotional wellness is the ability to successfully handle life's stresses and adapt to change and difficult times. It involves recognizing and respecting your feelings, needs, and wants. A balanced emotional state acquires self-awareness, self-regulation, motivation, empathy, and adept social skills. Emotional wellness should not be mistaken as the absence of emotional struggle. In reality, it endorses acknowledging uncomfortable emotions, understanding their origins, and using effective strategies to move through them.

Individuals with solid emotional wellness can express their feelings clearly and comfortably, rather than ignoring or denying them. They also understand that every emotion has a certain value and purpose, whether it's joy showing satisfaction, sadness expressing a need for support, anger indicating a boundary being crossed, or fear alerting to potential danger.

12.2. Developing a Personal Emotional Wellness Plan

A personal emotional wellness plan is a roadmap to identity, manage, and express feelings in a constructive way. It revolves around improving emotional literacy for everyone within the household. Below are some steps to consider while crafting your emotional wellness plan:

1. Reflection: Ponder on feelings you have difficulty managing. Are there certain triggers or patterns you can identify?

2. Building Emotional Vocabulary: Seek to expand your emotional vocabulary. This is particularly paramount with children, teaching them that there's more to their feelings than just 'happy', 'sad', 'angry', or 'afraid'.

3. Practicing Emotional Identification: Try to identify and label emotions in daily life. This promotes emotional awareness and control.

4. Developing Coping Strategies: Learn and practice different strategies to cope with challenging emotions. These can include deep breathing, mindfulness, or even physical activity.

12.3. Conveying Emotions: The Power of Effective Communication

Effective communication is vital in emotion management. You need to listen actively, validate emotions - your own and your children's. Instead of dismissing feelings, genuine interests help build trust and confidence. Encourage articulating emotions appropriately and reinforce the understanding that no emotion is wrong. Encourage words over actions, enabling children to express their feelings through conversation rather than acting out.

12.4. Promoting Emotional Wellness in Kid

Fostering emotional wellness in children is valuable for their development. Begin by modeling healthy emotional habits: children learn through observation. Also, validate your child's feelings: regardless of how trivial their concerns may appear.

1. Practice Empathy: Empathy is not about solving your child's problems, but rather expressing understanding and reassurance that they're not alone.

2. Teach Problem-solving: Problem-solving skills are crucial for handling scenarios that stir potent feelings. Show them how to identify a problem, think of multiple solutions, weigh each, and decide on the best one.

3. Foster a Positive Outlook: Teach children to maintain a healthy perspective towards life, viewing problems as opportunities rather than dead-ends.

12.5. The Value of Resilience: Aiding Emotional Wellness

Resilience, the ability to bounce back from adversity, is a crucial element in maintaining emotional wellness over a lifetime. It involves healthy habits and supports that help us navigate through life's ups and downs. It's taking care of physical well-being, maintaining a positive outlook, offering self-care, seeking help when needed, and fostering connections.

12.6. Adopting a Lifelong Learning Approach for Emotional Wellness

Emotional wellness is about acknowledging a constantly evolving emotional landscape, and the necessity of lifelong learning. Just like your child, you too continue to grow and evolve every day. Reach out to mental health professionals, attend workshops, join parenting communities for mutual learning and upliftment, read, reflect and question. Just remember, it's a journey, not a destination.

Emotional wellness is a crucial part of life and a core determinant of overall wellbeing. It involves recognizing, understanding, expressing, and managing feelings. Emotionally well individuals are better equipped to face life's challenges, build strong relationships, and recover from setbacks. Understanding and developing personal and familial emotional wellness will pave the way for a happier, healthier household.